AMAZING ARTS.

BY,
DEEPA MATHAR.

CONTENTS

ACKNOWLEDGEMENT.

I ACKNOWLEDGE THAT ALL THE INFORMATION GIVEN BY ME IS TRUE. IN THE ARTS TOPIC, THERE IS A DISCUSSION OF VARIOUS TYPES OF ARTS LIKE MAURYAN ART, GUPTA ARTS, INDIAN ARTS, WORLD ARTS. IN THE NEXT TOPIC, THERE IS A DISCUSSION OF DIFFERENT TYPES OF FLOWERS. THERE IS ANOTHER TOPIC OF LARGEST RIVERS OF THE WORLD.

ART AND ARCHITECTURE OF THE WORLD.

Art is the creation of different types of work with beauty and attraction in it. In other words, art is the creation of beauty. Beauty and creativity are closely related to each other and they both are the characteristics of art. Art is classified in two types - natural arts and artificial arts. The Indian art consists of paintings, sculpture, stone, seals, potteries and architecture. Arts are also of various types and qualities. Most of the arts contains paintings in it. Some arts are found in writing forms. Art and beauty are inter related. In the same way, art and creativity are also inter related. Art is found in coins, Walls, sculptures and architectures.

NATURAL ART

The arts which are available thousands of years ago are called natural arts. Many of these arts are designed in the walls of temples are natural arts. These arts are of those times when the world starts or we can say in very early period. But nowadays, these types of arts are too old with the changing times.

ARTIFICIAL ART

These are man-made arts in early times. These arts were made by ancestral people. Arts are also found in with figures of humans. Art is also seen in the simple coins of ancient times. We also see art in the development of civilization. Art is also classified in other designed arts, decorated arts and hand-made arts. When the art is designed it looks attractive, when the art is decorated, it looks amazing and when it is hand-made it looks wonderful. Most of the arts have paintings in them. Art is done by the artists and an artist wants the good price for their arts and architectural work.

Art and Architecture both are directly related to the histories of the world. History relates to the kingdoms and their dynasties. These arts and architecture shows the choice, preferences, styles and the interests of various Kingdoms. The arts of different kingdoms varies from each other due to their food habits, Languages and regions. Their social and economic policies are also different from each other which easily reflects in the art and architecture of a particular place. In India also,there were many kings and their dynasties ruled over centuries. So their art and architecture are easily found In every historical Places with their historical arts. These places are the main attractions for all the people. Every art and architecture shows the different intellectual level of different artists like what things they use. At the time of production of specific art and in its design work. All the other information are easily found in the palaces of different kingdoms. It also shows their royal luxuries which defined the Status and beauty of their lives.

INDIAN ART

Indian art is a term used in the history of India specially in the regions of India.The Indian art has a rich and complex history. India was the only major Asian culture. Archaeologists have found the evidences of rock art. These are the drawings on rock. The oldest example is Bhimbetka petro-glyphs which is found in central India. It is estimated that about 1300 rock arts are there. There are many painted rock shelters in central India. The ancient art of central India looks very attractive. The rock shelters are near the vindhya mountain range.The paintings have common scenes of human life and hunting scenes of human with their different stone implements which were used by the ancient people of India.

The Indus valley civilization is also very popular. In this civilization, small terracotta and bronze figures are used. These figures depict humans , animals like cows, monkeys and dancing posts of humans. There are many sculpture pieces made by the religious artists of India. Hinduism shows many art creation from centuries. There are sculptures of Shiva and other deities are also present in the temples of Hindus. Under the Mughal empire, Taj Mahal was built by Shah Jahan. The British established art schools shows European styles. Contemporary Indian art is an international art.

TYPES AND STYLES

Traditional Indian art has a religious character. Hinduism and Buddhism are very common in Indian art. Many Hindu temples have very distinctive towers in the form of truncated pyramids. The other famous art is Mauryan art. There is a Mauryan stone sculpture in the capital of Bihar.The place is Pataliputra . The other famous symbol of India which is India's national emblem is the Sarnath four lions under the kingdom of Ashoka.This art is placed in the museum now. The Mauryan empire is from 322 B.C to 185 B.C. The Emperor Ashoka adopted the religion of Buddhism and during his forty years of reign, he made large stupas from the life of Buddha. The other famous arts are pillars of Ashoka. It showed very confident and bold mature style. Mauryan sculpture and architecture both are very famous which is flourished under the kingdom of Ashoka. This sculpture and art has very fine polish and beauty given to the stone . The artists made these sculptures with their high artistic techniques. These art techniques are very rarely seen in other arts of India. It is an exceptional art. These artists of Mauryan empire have higher level of creativity in the art of sculptures. Many yaksha statues are also found in India. Nowadays, only few statues remained in good condition.

BUDDHIST ART

The Buddhist art also has good quantity of sculpture . Some places are Sanchi and Amravati.The Stupas were surrounded by ceremonial fences with four profusely carved ornamental gateways facing the directions . These are in the stones. One of the famous is 'The Great Sanchi Stupa'which was founded by Mauryan emperor Ashoka during his empire. The walls of the stupa can be heavily decorated with reliefs illustrating the life of Mahatma Buddha. The Ajanta caves are also very popular. There are iconic figures of Buddha and Bodhisattvas.

These arts are influenced by Hindus and jain religious figurative art . The figures are also influenced by Greco – Buddhist art. The Buddhist sculptures have epigraphs. These epigraphs are written in Brahmi characters which are found in divine places. In Satvahana dynasty who ruled in central India made stupas, temples and prayer halls. Other important stupa is Amravati Stupa. Stupas are religious monuments .These are built on burial mounds. It contains relics beneath a solid dome. Stupas in India are different in their size, design and structure .The designs are based on Mandala. It is a group of cosmos to Buddhism. Ancient Indian caves are also sacred places because holy men and monks lived there. A chaitya was constructed from a cave. Satvahana people also made the images on stone in Buddhism. They create ideal images of tools like chisels, hammers, and compasses with iron points which is based on the geometry and geology.They also have coins in their arts. The coins are usually in copper and lead but later silver coinsCame into use. These coins show the pictures of rulers and inscriptions written on it. Under the Kushan empire, Kushan art was developed. The physical form of the Buddha and his Boddhisattvas well designed with solid and muscular body with swelling chests arms and abdomen.

GUPTA ART

This art is one of the major art of north India including the religious art. The works are religious in the Ajanta caves. The deities are shown in this art mainly Buddha figure and Jain Tirthankara figures. These figures are very large in scale. This is the golden age of India.One of the art is Chola bronze statue of Nataraja in the metropolitan museum of art in New Delhi .There is a famous small bronze male dancer in Mohen jo daro and Harappa Civilization. These figures are very rarely found and outnumbered by pottery figurines and Stone seals. The Elephanta caves are also there. Large scale of sculpture is religious. The Chola Paintings were discovered in the year 1931 are from the temple of Brihadeshvara at Thanjavur.The modern Indian art is considered to begun in 19 century.

Miniature paintings- These are the Mughal paintings .These are very popular also in nowadays. These paintings include all the things like humans, animals, plants and other things of the world. These paintings look very attractive and beautiful.

Jewellery – There are high quality of gemstones that are available which are used in the jewellery of the arts. Jewellery is one of the main part of an art. Firstly, these jewelleries were made in the Indus valley civilization.

ART OF SOUTH INDIA

CHAARMINAR – It is located in the city of Hyderabad. It is an example of Indo – Islamic architecture. It was constructed during the period of the Delhi kingdoms. Qutab minar and Alai minar are other examples. The Mughal architecture started from the Tomb of Humayun. But the Mughal empire is famous for its unique Taj Mahal. It is said the king Shah Jahan who made Taj Mahal for his wife. It takes twenty two years to make all the arts of Taj Mahal. It is the symbol of true love.

BRIHADESHWARA TEMPLE

This is a temple of Hindus. This temple is dedicated to Lord Shiva. It is also called Rajrajeshvaram in Tamil nadu. It is located in the district of Thanjavur .This temple is situated near the banks of river Kaveri. It is one of the largest and famous temples of India. It was built by Tamil king Raja Raja Chola. The temple is also a part of the UNESCO World Heritage. There is a big statue of Nandi in the temple. The entire temple is made of granite. It is one of the tourist attractions in Tamil Nadu.

GOLGUMBAZ

It is the monument of Bijapur located in the Karnataka. It is made by the king Adil Shah.The monument derives its name from Gola Gummat which means a circular dome. It is one of the significant monuments of South India. The Deccan sultanates have five dynasties and their architecture was a regional variant of Indo Islamic architecture. It is largely influenced by the style of Delhi Sultanates and it is also inspired by Mughal architecture and some arts of Persia and Central Asia. The other examples are Iron Pillar, Standing Buddha and Ashoka's queen.

Humayun Tomb is famous for large onion domes and it is surrounded by the gardens. It also contains delicate ornamental work which includes pachin karu decorative work.It is the combination of Indian and Persian architecture. It is one of the famous places. Humayun's wife Hamida Banu Begum commissioned the building of this tomb for her husband in the 15 century.

THE NORTH INDIAN FORTS

AGRA FORT

It is one of the important architecture of India. It was built by the Mughal king, Akbar.

RED FORT

Red fort is also one of the Mughal architecture. It was constructed over ten years from 1638 to 1648. It was made when Shah Jahan shifted the capital from Agra to Delhi. It is also one of the most famos places to visit by all the peoples. There is an audio show related to the history of Red fort seen to viewers. The historical sounds and voices are easily heard in this show. Many people go to hear it.

Taj Mahal is also one of the North Indian forts.

The Maratha Architecture has examples like Lal Mahal and Shaniwar Wada. The Maratha ruled from 17 to 19 century. Al l the Indo Islamic architecture are very famous.

THE RAJPUT ARCHITECTURE

This architecture is from Rajasthan and it is a regional variant of style of Rajasthan. Rajasthan is popular for its forts and palaces of different Rajput kings. All the places of forts and palaces of Rajasthan are famous for its tourist attractions. The group of six Forts built by the Rajput kingdoms during the medieval world are City Palace, Hawa Mahal, Chittor Fort, Rambagh Palace, Fort , Mehrangarh Fort and Jal Mahal. Lalgarh palace is in Bikaner, Monsoon palace is located in Udaipur and Umaid Bhavan palace is located in Jodhpur.

HAWA MAHAL

Hawa Mahal is a palace of winds. It looks like a honey comb of a beehive with its 953 intricate windows. The main purpose for these windows is to facilitate the royal ladies to watch outside the Mahal. The shape of the building is like a crown. This was built by Maharaja Sawai Pratap Singh who was a major devotee of Lord Krishna. It looks very attractive and beautiful.

GUJARAT ARCHITECTURE

Kutch is the city of Gujarat having many places to visit. One of the palace is Vijay Vilas Palace. It was made by Maharaja Jadeja of Kutch .It is located on the sea beach of Mandvi in Gujarat. It is an example of Indo sarcenic architecture. The other palace is Laxmi Vilas Palace of Vadodara. It also contains sarcenic architecture and it was built by Maharaja Sayajirao Gaekwad in 1890. Some of the tourist attractions are Aina Mahal and Prag Mahal of Bhuj in Kutch of Gujarat. Dolat Nivas Palace in Ider and Art Deo Palace in Morbi are some of the palaces of Gujarat.

RANI KI VAV

It was made in the 11 century A.D. It was made by the queen Udaymati.

KONARK TEMPLE

The king Narsimhadeva with his 1200 artisans built this magic Konark temple. There are 12 wheels at the base of the temple which are sundials that denote the time from morning to evening.

KUMBHALGARH FORT

It is the fort in Rajasthan which is famous for its art. It was built by the Kumbha. It is 82 km from Udaipur. The walls of Kumbhalgarh are the second largest wall in the world which rank after the Great Wall of China.

CENOTAPHS

These cenotaphs are mostly found in chatir forms. They include ahai cenotaphs and Badabagh near Jaisalmer. Chaurasi Khambo Ki Chatri and Bundi are other examples.

ROMAN ARTS

These arts are practised by the Romans. It includes sculpture, bronze has decorative art including meta l work, jewellery and ivory carving. Roman art has very fine jewellery ,funery sculpture, Perspective Drawing, caricature, genre, portrait painting, landscape painting and architectural painting.

ANCIENT CLASSICAL ARTS

It relates to greek architecture and art. It is concerned with geometry and symmetry. A religious Art is characterised by domes, rounded arches and mosaics from the eastern Roman empire in the fourth century. In Greek art , Haphaestus was the god of artisans and sculpture geometric , archaic, classical and hellenistic. Major constituents of art include literature which has fiction, drama, poetry and prose. The performing arts are dance, music and theatre. The visual arts are painting, drawing, film making and architecture. Visual arts also contains ceramics, sculpting and photography. The oldest portrait of Jesus is found in Syria and shows him as a beardless young man of authoritative and dignified bearing.

The God, Jesus who was the founder of Christianity is depicted dressed in the style of a young philosopher with close cropped hair and wearing a tunic and pallium. These are the signs of good breeding in Greeco-Roman society.

Modern art includes aristic work produced during the period roughly from 1860 to 1970 which denotes the style and philosophy of the art produced during that era. The Monalisa, is an oil painting by an Italian artist and inventor and writer Leonardo da vinci. The piece features a portrait of a seated woman set against an imagery landscape. It is also one of the valuable

paintings of the world.

FLORAL BEAUTY.

Indian flowers.

A flower has good fragrance. Evey flower has different colours which are natural. Every flowers

Shape is different from other flowers. In this way, flowers are very beautiful and attracrive.

name of indian flower is Lotus.Another name is Kamal in hindi.It is a sacred lotus. The scientific

name is Nelumba and Nucifera.It is found in south easterb Asian countries.It is also cultivated in

Australia.It is found in India. It is also found in Europe, Japan and America.It is usually found in places

Like ponds, lakes and artificial pools.It is 1.5 cm long and there are 30 petals in lotus. It is termed as

Padma.

There are many types of flowers. It is estimated that there are 1800 flowers.

Calla lilies.

Daisies.

Gardenias.

Orchids.

Roses.

The names of some flowers are-

Carnations.

Irises.

Lavender.

Roses.

Tulips.

Sunflower.

Orchids.

Gardenias.

Carnations.

These ruffly flowers are perfect for the love relations.

Irises

Purple is the colour of royalty. This flower stands for faithand hope.

Lavender.

It is a sweet smelling flower which is given to others.

Roses

Roses are the flowers which are the symbol of love between two persons.

Tulips

Tulips are very beautiful flowers. Having a great natural design.

Sunflowers.

Sunflower is extra ordinary flower which always grows and stands towards sunlight.

Gardenias

Gardenias are also special kind of flowers. The flowers are divided into four colours-

Focal flowers

Filter flowers.

Greenery or line flowers.

Flowers are divided into two types-

Monocots

Dicots.

All the pink flowers like flowers of cherry blossom,flower of cherry blossom, light pink cherry.

It is called that red flowers are so rarest.The eulophia obtuse is a highly rare species of orchid with very beautiful flowers.

The study of flowers is called floriculture.

Pomology.

Spermology.

Anthology.

Pomology- It is a branch of botany which analyses and cultivates fruits.

Spermology – It is a study of seeds.

Anthology - This is a study of flowers and flowering plants.

Floriculture – The study of flowers is called floriculture.

A flower known as blossom. It has the reproductive structure. It is found in flowering plants.

The pollination has two types –

Self pollination.

It happens when the pollen grain from the anther is deposited on the stigma of the same flower.

Cross pollination.

It happens when the pollen grains from the anther is deposited on the stigma of the same flower.

Cross pollination

It is the transfer of pollen from from the anther of the flower to the stigma of another flower.

These flowering plants are of same species. Flowers contain sporangia. In the process of fertilisation, ovary of the flower develops into fruit.It contains seeds also. Flowers are very beautiful and looks attractive. Flowers also have very good smelling nature.

Species of flowers

Sweet pea

Yarrow

California poppy.

Primrose

Common daisy

Flax

Lily of the lily

Poinsetia

Sacred lotus

Platycodon grandifloras

Cornflower

Common poppy

Snapdragon

Black- eyed susan

Titan arum

Crown imperial

Summer liler

Silver ragvort

Cantrbury bells

Chives

Wild carrot

Tropical white morning

Barberton daisy

Yellow archangel

Cardial flower

Blue milk

Sea thrift

Hyssop

Borage

Wishbone flower

Snow in summer

Fennel

Chicory

Shoe black poppy

Weed anemone

Sweet alyssum

Common ivory

Butterfly weed

Linum perenne

Red valerian

Dame's rocket

Sweet William

Jack in the pulpit

Bee orchid

Maidan pink

Common zinnia

Common bluebell

In this way, there are four lakh species of the flowering plants.

ANCIENT ARTS

The first oldest form of prehistoric art are petroglyphs, which appeared throughout the world During the lower paleolithic age. Ancient arts refers to many types of art produced by advanced Cultures of ancient societies with some form of writing such as those of China, India, Persia, Palestine, Egypt, Greece and Rome.

ROMAN ARTS

These arts are practised by the Romans. It includes sculpture, bronze statues and marble statues. The fine art consists of paintings and vase painting.It also has decorative art including metal work. It also has jewellery and ivory carving.Roman art has fine jewellery,metalwork,funery sculpture, Perspective drawing, caricature,genre, portrait painting, landscape painting and architectural Painting.

LARGEST RIVERS OF THE EARTH

A river is a water which is flowing downwards .Rivers contains fresh water, soil water, stone water

River is a part of water cycle .The river water evaporates in the sunlight due to the heat of the sun,

then it forms clouds and clouds again falls in the form of water specially in the form of river water.

The longest rivers of the world are

Nile river.

Amazon river.

Yangtze river .

Missouri river.

Mississippi river.

Yukon river.

Arkansas river.

Rio grenade river.

St. Lawrence river.

Colorado river.

Ohio river.

Red river.

Brazos river.

Brazos river.

Snake river.

Platte river.

Pecas river.

Canadian river.

Tennesse river.

North Canadian river.

Mobile river.

Kansa river.

Yellow stone river.

Milk river.

Kansas river.

Hamilton river.

Cimarron river.

Rivers provide water for all the essential needs.

Nile is the biggest river.

RIVERS OF THE INDIA.

Ganga is the longest river of India.

The names of other rivers are −

Narmada river.

Tapi river.

Gidavari river.

Chenab river.

Ravi river.

Beas river.

Sutlej river.

Jhelum river.

Indus river.

Sabarmati river.

Mahi river.

Krishna river.

Mahanadi river.

These rivers have bigger importance in the life of the people of India.

One river is Lena river in Russia with kilometres 4294 and the length of the river is 2736.

The next river is Argun river which is located in Russia, China and Mongolia with a kilometres

of 4444 with 2763 miles. The other river is Chambeshi river located in Central Africa with a

Kilometres 4700 and a alength of 2922 miles.The other river is Irtysh river located in Russia,

China, Mongolia and Kazakhastan with kilometres 5410 and a length of 3364. The next river is

Located in China named Yellow river. The other river is Yenisei Angara. The river is longest river

in Russia and Mongolia. The next river is Mississippi and Missouri located in United States of

 America. The other river is Nile river located in North East Africa with a kilometres 6853 with a

Length of 4258. The other river is Amazon river is located in South America with a kilometres

of kilometres of 6992 and a length of 4344.

In India, people worship the rivers and see them sacred rivers.and see them as sacred and

Religious rivers. These rivers have bigger importance in the lives of the people.The deepest river in

India is Bhagirathi, named Ganga.The Indus river is also called the Sindha which is the longest river in

Asia. India's most dangerous river is Vishwamitra in Vadodara Gujarat. The other major rivers of

India are Brahmaputra, Yamuna, Kali, Gomati,Chambal, Betwa, Ken, Tons, Ghagra, Gandak, Koshi,

Mahanadi, Tamsa, Son, Bagmati, Meghna,Krishna and Kaveri.

The rivers in Arabian sea are-

Sutlej river.

Beas river.

Parbati river.

Chenab river.

Ravi river.

Jhelum river.

Neelum river.

Dras river.

Shingo river.

Yapoli river.

Markha river.

Khurma river.

Zanskar river.

Suru river.

Doda river.

Hanley river.

Marutsudha river.

DESIGNER JEWELLERIES.

The jewellery has full attraction and beauty. The jewellery has many types like Diamond jewellery, Pearl jewellery, decorative jewellery, shining jewellery, Mirror jewellery, Colourful jewellery, Simple jewellery, Hard jewellery or heavty jewellery, Light jewellery. The jewellery forms with rings, necklaces, earrings, bracelets, hair accessories, pendants and bangles. Jemstone jewelleries are also very popular.There are preciousmetals in jewellery.The jewellery is derived from jewel.

DECORATIVE JEWELLERY

These jewelleries are full decorated with many shining and colourful things which are used in jewellery.

SHINING JEWELLERY

The shining jewellery has full shining. The shining reflects in mirrors and other things.

DIAMOND JEWELLERY

The diamond jewellery are more costly.The jewelleries are famous for their shining and their decorations.

COLOURFUL JEWELLERY

These jewelleries contains colours like green, red, pink, blue and orange.

MIRROR JEWELLERY

These jewelleries contains small pieces of mirrors. These are also like shining jewelleries.They have more reflections in it.

IMPORTANCE OF JEWELLERY

Jewellery represents wealth, powerand prestige. It adds very positive things in your identity.

TYPES OF JEWELLERY

Antique jewellery.

Bead jewellery.

Bridal jewellery.

Fashion jewellery.

Filigree jewellery.

Handmade jewellery.

Kundan jewellery.

GOLDEN AND SILVER JEWELLERY.

Golden jewellery- The golden jewellery contains beautiful golden ornamental things and many designer jewels. This jewelleries are more famous as compared to other jewelleries because it is a symbol of love and prestige or power.People mostly like golden jewelleries.These golden jewelleries are available in many forms like kada, bracelets, earrings, hand rings, necklaces, pins, pendants, and even payals.

SILVER JEWELLERY

These types of jewellery are easily worn by the people because they are less costly. These jewelleries are also available in kada, bracelets, earrings, hand rings, pins and pendants.

TYPES OF JEWELLERY

Antique jewellery.

Temple jewellery.

Bead jewellery.

Bridal jewellery.

Fashion jewellery.

Filigree jewellery.

Handmade jewellery.

Kundan jewellery.

Polki jewellery.

There are many types of jewellery like golden, silver and gold plaes jewellery.The traditional dancers

 use ornamental jewellery in dances like Kathak, Bharatnatyam and Odissi.

ANTIQUE JEWELLERY

The term antique jewellery are used interchangeably..The jewellery is considered to be antique

when it is thousands of years ago.

TEMPLE JEWELLERY

Temple jewellery is the name given to the jewellery worn by Bharatnatyam.The list of ornaments

are-

Hair and head ornaments.

Neck ornaments.

Arm ornaments.

Hand ornaments.

Body ornaments.

Feet ornaments.

There are many other tyoes of jewelleries-

Prayer jewellery

Japa malas

Prayer beads

Prayer rope

Rosary beads

Puzzle jewellery

Puzzle ring

Signet ring

Thumb ring

Pledge pins

Military dry tags.

There are different types of art jewellery –

These tyoes of jewelleries include Crowns, Diaden, Corolla, Mekuta, Kokoshnik, Schent,Tiara,

Earrings, Ear cuff, Fascinator,Hair pins Hatpin and Sarpech.

There are Many types of neck jewellery –

Choker

Necklace

Pendant

Chain

Bolotu

Tore

Bangle

Bracelet

Friendship bracelet

Armlet

Cuff links.

There are many hand jewelleries –

Class ring

Engagement ring

Navarat ring

Promrise ring

Pre engagement ring

Wedding ring

Slave bracelet

There are other body ornaments-

Brooch

Belly chain

Body piercing jewellery

Chatelaine

Body piercing jewellery.

There are many feet jewelleries-

Ankle

Toe ring.

TRADITIONAL JEWELLERY OF INDIA

The traditional jewellery has its own importance.It looks very beautiful.The jewellery of traditional look is very good.The Indian jewellery is very old. The temples of South Inia ,Odissa and central India looks very attractive and graceful.

JEWELLERY OF MUGHAL EMPEROR

There are Mughal rings, Mughal empire traditional jewelleries . It also includes hand ornaments and earrings. All the types of jewelleries are important in any kind of occasions and specially in celebrating festivals.